For Anneliese, whose fire and courageous spirit are unbeatable.
Keep going, my girl.
—A.C.K.

To my sister Christie
—J.S.

Unbeatable Betty: The First Female Olympic Track & Field Gold Medalist
Text copyright © 2020 by Allison Crotzer Kimmel
Illustrations copyright © 2020 by Joanie Stone
ISBN 978-0-06-289607-0

The artist used Photoshop to create the digital illustrations for this book.
Typography by Rachel Zegar
20 21 22 23 24 SCP 10 9 8 7 6 5 4 3 2 1
❖
First Edition

UNBEATABLE BETTY

THE FIRST FEMALE OLYMPIC TRACK & FIELD GOLD MEDALIST

By Allison Crotzer Kimmel

Illustrated by Joanie Stone

HARPER

An Imprint of HarperCollins Publishers

Betty Robinson knew two things for sure: She could run, and she needed to catch a train.

So she ran.

When Betty took her seat on the train, her legs weren't even tired. Across from her, Mr. Charles Price, the science teacher and boys' track coach from her high school, stared.

"I know a runner when I see one," he said.

The next day, Coach Price asked Betty to run in the school hallway. Betty's sprint was just short of the US indoor record.

"Could you do that again?" the coach asked.

She wasn't even wearing track shoes! He'd never coached a girl before—girls weren't supposed to run in 1928. But he asked Betty to join the boys' high school track team anyway. Betty had to run with the boys, but soon she'd be running past them.

At her first regional competition in Chicago, Betty thought of her hometown of Riverdale,
Illinois—its clotheslines, its backyards, and the streets she grew up running through. None of
them had been like this. But Coach Price had said all that matters is the runner and the track.
When the gun sounded to start the race, Betty's legs pumped all the way to the finish line.
She came in second to the American women's record holder.
Turns out Elizabeth Robinson could run with the best of them.

Only four months later, Betty was headed to the first Olympics in which women were allowed to run. Betty was only sixteen when the boat docked in Amsterdam. She had come to the 1928 Olympics to prove that female bodies weren't too weak for track.

On the day of the 100-meter race, the Olympic crowd's cheering vibrated from Betty's head all the way to her toes. Running had made her toenails fall off!

As she crouched at the starting line, she noticed Canadian Fanny Rosenfeld. Fanny was one of the world's fastest women, and the champion expected to win gold. Betty remembered Coach Price's advice. She was the runner, and no matter where the track was, it was hers and hers alone.

Betty fixed her eyes on the track ahead. She ran until she crossed the finish line at 12.2 seconds. Fanny crossed at 12.3 seconds.

In less than thirteen seconds, Betty Robinson became the first female ever to win an Olympic gold medal in track and field, beating out the favorite, Fanny.

Betty watched the American flag rise high above her. She felt goose bumps when she heard the national anthem. And Betty, who everyone called "Smiling Betty," cried. Betty cried not because girls are weak but because she'd proven they were strong.

America celebrated its "Golden Girl," Betty, with parades, and Betty celebrated by setting records across the country. And when she crossed each finish line, her smile remained. There was nothing this girl, this *runner*, couldn't do.

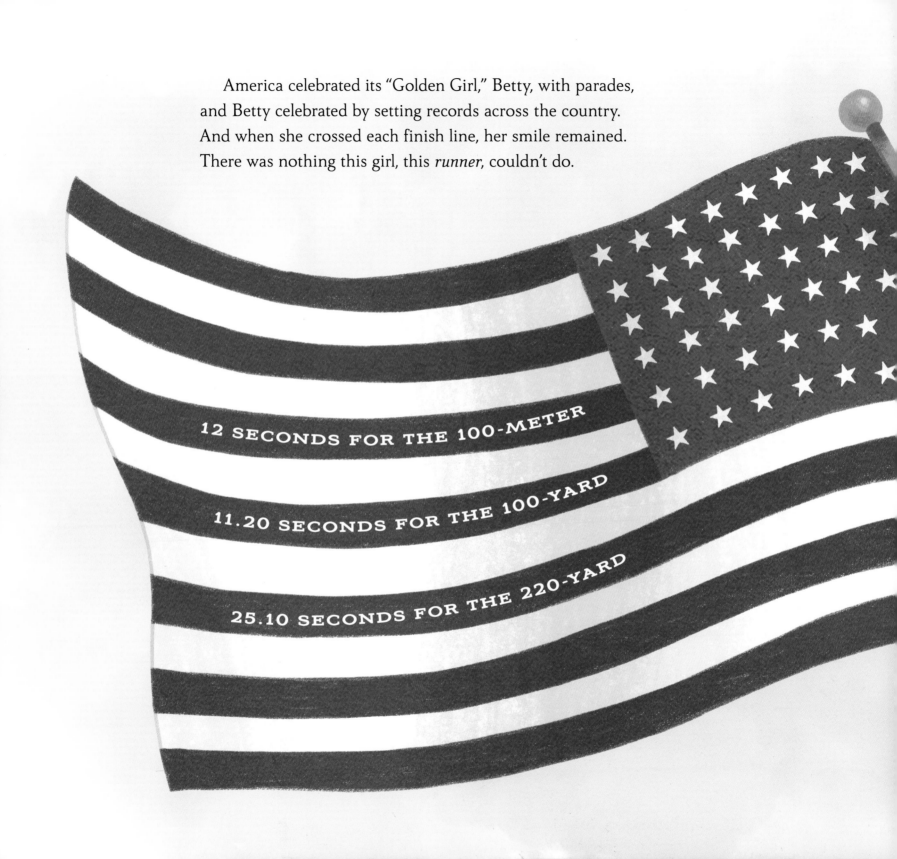

12 SECONDS FOR THE 100-METER

11.20 SECONDS FOR THE 100-YARD

25.10 SECONDS FOR THE 220-YARD

Yet she was focused on a distant track—the one she planned to meet in the 1932 Olympics in Los Angeles.

Betty trained harder.

Betty ran faster.

She was ready.

But she wasn't ready for the toughest competition of her life. On June 28, 1931, Betty went aboard a biplane and strapped on a flying helmet just like Amelia Earhart's. The plane dipped in and out of the clouds that stretched like a track without a finish line.

Suddenly, Betty felt a jolt.
The motor had stalled.
The last thing Betty remembered was the ground rushing toward her.

Her left leg was crushed. They thought she was dead until the undertaker discovered Betty was still alive. At the hospital, her parents stayed by her side. They knew Betty was a fighter.

Seven weeks later, when Betty awoke from a coma, she could not bend her knee. The doctors had put a silver rod and pins into her crushed leg. Her left leg was now shorter than the other. Pain shot through her like the sound from a starter's pistol. They said she would never walk again.

They said, "Forget running. Forget Los Angeles. Forget the Olympics."

But Betty could not.
All she could think of was her and her track.
When reporters interviewed her, she said, "Of course I am going to run again."

Betty knew this was simply a different kind of track she faced.
And all that had ever mattered had been her and the track.
She used a wheelchair for just four months.

Then Betty stood.

Then Betty walked.

And finally, again she ran.

It took her two years to relearn to stand, walk, and then run, but Betty was headed back to the Olympics.

She learned she could not run as she once had. The pin in her leg meant she could not crouch into the starting position for the 100-meter dash. That had been her race. It had always been just Betty and her 100 meters of track.

But if she wanted another gold medal, she would have to run the relay for the United States. She'd take off standing, waiting for a teammate to pass her the baton. Betty wanted gold, so she agreed. She would share her track with fellow Americans Harriet Bland, Annette Rogers, and Helen Stephens.

At the 1936 Berlin Olympics their biggest competitor was the German team. The Germans had a habit of setting records. And now they were favored to win.

As everyone predicted, the Germans were soon in the lead. Betty had overcome a train, a plane, and a wheelchair to become an Olympian.

She looked down at her leg, its ache constant, and she knew this race was different.

But one thing was still the same—it was just Betty and her track.

Betty saw Helen reaching for the baton. The fireworks in her leg exploded as she pressed in toward her teammate. She leaned into the headwind. She felt the ground below tremble. Betty let her arms pump and the limp she could not hide propel her down the track.

She passed her baton to Helen, and then suddenly there was a gasp across the stadium. . . . The last German runner dropped her baton as Helen galloped over the finish line.

Betty had finally gotten gold again, but this time it had been with her teammates Helen, Harriet, and Annette.

When Betty Robinson stood atop the Olympic podium with one leg shorter than the other, she did not cry. And for just a moment, she forgot the pain in her leg.

Betty stood proudly before the German crowd applauding
America's Golden Girl, imperfections and all.

AUTHOR'S NOTE

Soon after her miraculous second stand on top of the Olympic podium, Betty retired from running. The Berlin Games held more than just Betty and her relay team's amazing win. Those Games were made famous by Betty's friend, American men's track and field star Jesse Owens, who won four astonishing medals in Berlin, dismantling Hitler's idelology of Aryan superiority. The Olympic Games were also put on hold until 1948 as Hitler and his Nazi army stormed across Europe, causing World War II.

Betty held records in the 100-meter, 100-yard, and 220-yard dashes. Betty's successes on the Olympic track paved the way for later female track stars such as Wilma Rudolph, Florence Griffith Joyner, and Allyson Felix. Betty went on to give speeches and fight for women's sports programs. The US Olympic Committee inducted Betty into its Hall of Fame in 1977. Betty was the first woman from any country to win an Olympic gold medal in track and field, and she is still the youngest 100-meter champion in Olympic history. Her Olympic debut was only her fourth competitive race ever. Though Betty never gained the fame of later track stars, she continued to be active in track as a timer and coach, and she thought perhaps her best legacy was her children and grandchildren, who survived her after her death on May 18, 1999.

Betty Robinson, courtesy of the Robinson-Schwartz family

During a time when women weren't supposed to be athletes, young Betty proved women could compete and that women were made to run. Five years after nearly dying in a plane crash, Betty Robinson stood on the Olympic podium once again. Betty showed that it takes more than talent to become and stay a champion. Her legacy of hard work and determination remind everyone that a dream is within reach if we run as fast as we can and work as hard as we can to catch it.

SOURCES

Craven, Karen. "Olympic Gold Medalist Betty Robinson Schwartz." *Chicago Tribune*. www.articles
.chicagotribune.com/1999-05-20/news/9905200305_1_mrs-schwartz-betty-robinson-schwartz
-richard-schwartz.

Gergen, Joe. *The First Lady of Olympic Track: The Life and Times of Betty Robinson*. Evanston, IL:
Northwestern University Press, 2014.

Montillo, Roseanne. *Fire on the Track: Betty Robinson and the Triumph of the Early Olympic Women*. New
York: Crown, 2017.

Rosen, Karen. "Betty Robinson: The Olympic Gold Medalist Who 'Came Back from the Dead.'" Team
USA. April 28, 2015. www.teamusa.org/News/2015/April/28/Betty-Robinson-The-Gold-Medalist
-Who-Came-Back-From-the-Dead.

USA Track and Field. www.usatf.org/HallOfFame/TF/showBio.asp?HOFIDs=137.

LEARN MORE ABOUT BETTY!

www.bettyrobinson.org

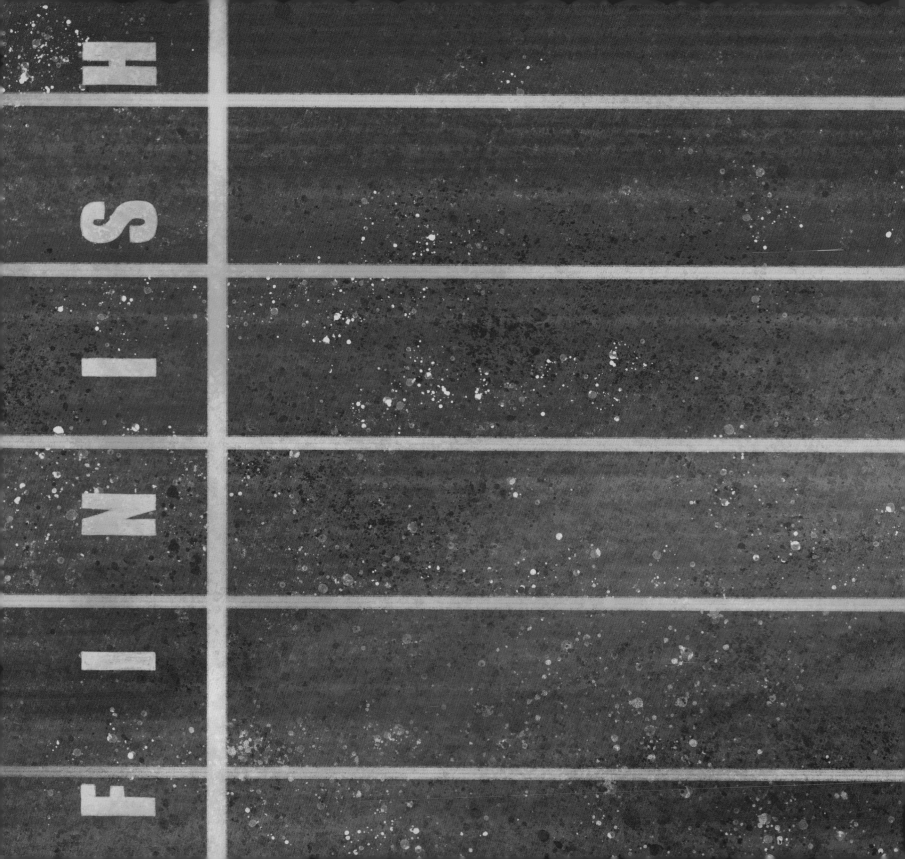